D0206561

May all beings
find a path to
peace.

Introduction
from
Jack Kornfield

Kathy Lane

Other Books by Jack Kornfield

Living Buddhist Masters (*Living Dharma*)
A Still Forest Pool (with Paul Breiter)
Seeking the Heart of Wisdom (with Joseph Goldstein)
Stories of the Spirit, Stories of the Heart / Soul Food
(with Christina Feldman)
Buddha's Little Instruction Book
Teachings of the Buddha
A Path with Heart
After the Ecstasy, the Laundry
The Wise Heart

The Art of
Forgiveness,
Lovingkindness,
and Peace

Jack Kornfield

BANTAM BOOKS
New York · Toronto · London · Sydney · Auckland

THE ART OF FORGIVENESS, LOVINGKINDNESS, AND PEACE
A Bantam Book

PUBLISHING HISTORY
Bantam hardcover edition published September 2002
Bantam hardcover reissue / June 2004
Bantam trade paperback edition / May 2008

Published by
Bantam Dell
A Division of Random House, Inc.
New York, New York

All rights reserved
Copyright © 2002 by Jack Kornfield

Book and cover design by David Bullen

Library of Congress Catalog Card Number: 20020218553

Bantam Books and the rooster colophon are registered trademarks of
Random House, Inc.

ISBN 978-0-553-38119-1

PRINTED IN THE UNITED STATES OF AMERICA

BVG   20 19 18 17 16 15 14 13 12 11

This simple book was written in the summer of 2001, shortly before the tragic events of terrorism and war swept another wave of violence over the world.

May the eternal truths and practices offered here be dedicated to the benefit of all who have suffered. May all beings find a path to peace.

Contents

You hold in your hand
an invitation:

To remember the transforming power
of forgiveness and lovingkindness.
To remember that no matter
where you are and what you face,
within your heart peace is possible.

The teachings in this book contain age-old understandings about love. They give simple and direct practices to help cultivate its qualities in your own heart.

This wisdom is essential for all who live in modern times.

The words of the Buddha offer this truth:

~ Hatred never ceases by hatred
  but by love alone is healed.
  This is the ancient and eternal law.

Often we find ourselves in conflicts that unsettle our peace of mind. We face difficult situations, and our problems can feel insurmountable.

Pain, anger, and fear can arise in ourselves, in families, in business, in communities, and between nations.

We would like to find a way out of the suffering.

Even in the worst situations, the heart can be free.

~ We who lived in the concentration camps
can remember those who walked through
the huts comforting others, giving away
their last piece of bread. . . . They may have
been few in number but they offer sufficient
proof that everything can be taken from
us but the last of human freedoms . . .
the freedom to choose our spirit in any
circumstance.

Viktor E. Frankl

Forgiveness and compassion are not sentimental or weak. They demand courage and integrity.

Yet they alone can bring about the peace we long for.

~   True love is not for the faint-hearted.

Meher Baba

Our innate wisdom knows this is true. When Buddhist texts address us as "O Nobly Born," they tell us we are all sons and daughters of the Buddha. Do not doubt your own basic goodness. In spite of all confusion and fear, you are born with a heart that knows what is just, loving, and beautiful.

In the words of Jungian analyst
Robert A. Johnson:

~ Curiously, people resist the noble aspects
  of their shadow more strenuously than they
  hide their dark sides. It is more disrupting
  to find that you have a profound nobility
  of character than to find out that you are
  a bum.

If we look at ourselves truthfully, we can feel the possibility of being more compassionate, more awake, more free.

~ If it were not possible to free the heart from entanglement in greed, hate, and fear, I would not teach you to do so.

Buddha

Anger, blame, conflict, and resentment arise from our fear. When we are afraid, our body tightens, our heart is constricted, our mind is possessed. We cannot live wisely.

Forgiveness releases us from the power of fear. It allows us to see with kindly eyes and rest in a wise heart.

Live in joy, in love,
even among those who hate.

Live in joy, in health,
even among the afflicted.

Live in joy, in peace,
even among the troubled.

Look within, be still.
Free from fear and attachment,
know the sweet joy of the way.

Buddha

How can we begin?

In any moment we can learn to let go of hatred and fear. We can rest in peace, love, and forgiveness. It is never too late.

Yet to sustain love we need to develop practices that cultivate and strengthen the natural compassion within us.

It is not enough to know that love and forgiveness are possible. We have to find ways to bring them to life.

~ The truth is we are not yet free; we have merely achieved the freedom to be free.

Nelson Mandela

Forgiveness

Traditionally
the work of the heart begins
with forgiveness.

Forgiveness is the necessary ground
for any healing.
First we need a wise understanding
of forgiveness.
Then we can learn how it is practiced,
how we may forgive both
ourselves and others.

Forgiveness is a letting go of past suffering and betrayal, a release of the burden of pain and hate that we carry.

Forgiveness honors the heart's greatest dignity. Whenever we are lost, it brings us back to the ground of love.

With forgiveness we become unwilling to attack or wish harm to another.

Whenever we forgive, in small ways at home, or in great ways between nations, we free ourselves from the past.

It is hard to imagine a world without forgiveness.
Without forgiveness life would be unbearable.

Without forgiveness our lives are chained,
forced to carry the sufferings of the past and
repeat them with no release.

Consider the dialogue between two former prisoners of war:

"Have you forgiven your captors yet?"
"No, never!"
"Well, then, they still have you in prison, don't they?"

We begin the work of forgiveness primarily for ourselves.

We may still be suffering terribly from the past while those who betrayed us are on vacation.

It is painful to hate. Without forgiveness we continue to perpetuate the illusion that hate can heal our pain and the pain of others.

In forgiveness we let go and find relief in our heart.

Even those in the worst situations, the conflicts and tragedies of Bosnia, Cambodia, Rwanda, Northern Ireland, or South Africa, have had to find a path to reconciliation. This is true in America as well. It is the only way to heal.

Sometimes this means finding the courage to forgive the unforgivable, to consciously release the heart from the clutches of another's terrible acts.

We must discover a way to move on from the past, no matter what traumas it held.

The past is over:

Forgiveness means giving up all hope of a better past.

Sometimes strong action may be needed for our defense. Let this be done with compassion or our own hatred will poison the response. We can meet the tragedies of the world with what Gandhi called "soul force."

~   If you want to see the heroic,
    look at those who can love
    in return for hatred.
    If you want to see the brave,
    look for those who can forgive.

Bhagavad Gita

Remember these truths:

FORGIVENESS IS NOT WEAK OR NAIVE.

Forgiveness requires courage and clarity; it is not naive. Mistakenly people believe that to forgive is to simply "forgive and forget," once and for all. This is not the wisdom of forgiveness.

FORGIVENESS DOES NOT HAPPEN QUICKLY.

For great injustice, coming to forgiveness
may include a long process of grief, outrage,
sadness, loss, and pain.

True forgiveness does not paper over what
has happened in a superficial way. It is not a
misguided effort to suppress or ignore our
pain. It cannot be hurried. It is a deep process
repeated over and over in our heart which
honors the grief and betrayal, and in its own
time ripens into the freedom to truly forgive.

FORGIVENESS DOES NOT FORGET,
NOR DOES IT CONDONE THE PAST.

Forgiveness sees wisely. It willingly acknowledges what is unjust, harmful, and wrong. It bravely recognizes the sufferings of the past, and understands the conditions that brought them about. There is a strength to forgiveness. When we forgive we can also say, "Never again will I allow these things to happen." We may resolve to never again permit such harm to come to ourselves or another.

FORGIVENESS DOES NOT MEAN THAT WE
HAVE TO CONTINUE TO RELATE TO THOSE
WHO HAVE DONE US HARM.

In some cases the best practice may be to end
our connection, to never speak to or be with
a harmful person again. Sometimes in the
process of forgiveness a person who hurt or
betrayed us may wish to make amends, but
even this does not require us to put ourselves
in the way of further harm.

In the end, forgiveness simply means never putting another person out of our heart.

If we could read the secret history of our enemies, we should see sorrow and suffering enough to disarm all hostility.

Henry Wadsworth Longfellow

Finding a way to extend forgiveness to ourselves is one of our most essential tasks.

Just as others have been caught in suffering, so have we.

If we look honestly at our life, we can see the sorrows and pain that have led to our own wrongdoing. In this we can finally extend forgiveness to ourselves; we can hold the pain we have caused in compassion. Without such mercy, we will live our own life in exile.

The pains of our past cannot be released — until we touch them with healing and forgiveness.

~ The truth about our childhood is stored up in our body, and although we can repress it, we can never alter it. Our intellect can be deceived, our feelings manipulated, our conceptions confused, and our body tricked with medication. But someday our body will present its bill, for it is as incorruptible as a child who, still whole in spirit, will accept no compromise or excuses, and it will not stop tormenting us until we stop evading the truth.

Alice Miller

We have all been blinded, we have all suffered. Pema Chödrön tells this story:

~ A young woman wrote about finding herself in a small town in the Middle East surrounded by people jeering, yelling, and threatening to throw stones at her and her friends because they were Americans.

Of course she was terrified, and what happened to her is important. Suddenly she identified with every person throughout history who had ever been scorned and hated. She understood what it was like to be despised for any reason: ethnic group, racial background, sexual preference, gender. Something cracked wide open and she stood in the shoes of millions of oppressed people and saw with a new perspective. She even understood her shared humanity with those who hated her. This sense of deep connection, of belonging to the same family, is the awakening of the great heart of compassion.

Alan Wallace illustrates this truth from the
  Tibetan teachings:

~   Imagine walking along a sidewalk with your
    arms full of groceries, and someone roughly
    bumps into you so that you fall and your
    groceries are strewn over the ground. As
    you rise up from the puddle of broken eggs
    and tomato juice, you are ready to shout
    out, "You idiot! What's wrong with you?
    Are you blind?" But just before you can
    catch your breath to speak, you see that
    the person who bumped into you actually
    is blind. He, too, is sprawled in the spilled
    groceries, and your anger vanishes in an
    instant, to be replaced by sympathetic
    concern: "Are you hurt? Can I help you up?"
    Our situation is like that. When we clearly
    realize that the source of disharmony and
    misery in the world is ignorance, we can
    open the door of wisdom and compassion.

No matter what has happened, we can always return to the greatness of the heart.

We have all heard stories about the mysterious power of compassion and forgiveness in the lives of others. Each time we are inspired by these accounts, we remember that we, too, can forgive.

Roberto de Vicenzo, the famous Argentine golfer, once won a tournament, and after receiving the check and smiling for the cameras, he went to the clubhouse and prepared to leave. Sometime later he walked alone to his car in the parking lot and was approached by a young woman. She congratulated him on his victory and then told him that her child was seriously ill and near death.

De Vicenzo was touched by her story and took out a pen and endorsed his winning check for payment to the woman. "Make some good days for the baby," he said as he pressed the check into her hand.

The next week he was having lunch in a country club when a PGA official came to his table. "Some of the guys in the parking lot last week told me you met a young woman there after you won the tournament." De Vicenzo nodded. "Well," said the official, "I have news for you. She's a phony. She's not married. She has no sick baby. She fleeced you, my friend."

"You mean there is no baby who is dying?" said de Vicenzo.

"That's right."

"That's the best news I've heard all week," said de Vicenzo.

The heart is released whenever we forgive
or are forgiven, even in the most painful
circumstances.

In ancient Hawaii, if a person had broken
a terrible taboo or was accused of a crime,
there was always a way out. No matter what
he had done, if he could get himself inside the
lava rock walls of Puahonua, the ocean-side
Temple of Refuge, the priests would offer a
ritual of purification and forgiveness. Then
he was allowed to return home unharmed.

In the temple of forgiveness, we are
reminded of our own goodness.

If only we could help each other build temples of forgiveness instead of prisons.

We can.

In our own hearts.

In the Babemba tribe of South Africa, when a person acts irresponsibly or unjustly, he is placed in the center of the village, alone and unfettered. All work ceases, and every man, woman, and child in the village gathers in a large circle around the accused individual. Then each person in the tribe speaks to the accused, one at a time, each recalling the good things the person in the center of the circle has done in his lifetime. Every incident, every experience that can be recalled with any detail and accuracy, is recounted. All his positive attributes, good deeds, strengths, and kindnesses are recited carefully and at length. This tribal ceremony often lasts for several days. At the end, the tribal circle is broken, a joyous celebration takes place, and the person is symbolically and literally welcomed back into the tribe.

The Sufi master Pir Vilayat Khan teaches us:

~   Overcome any bitterness that may have
    come because you were not up to the
    magnitude of the pain entrusted to you.
        Like the mother of the world who carries
    the pain of the world in her heart, you are
    sharing in a certain measure of that cosmic
    pain, and are called upon to meet it in joy
    instead of self-pity.

No matter how extreme the circumstances, a transformation of the heart is possible.

Once on the train from Washington to Philadelphia, I found myself seated next to an African American man who had worked for the State Department in India but had quit to run a rehabilitation program for juvenile offenders in the District of Columbia. Most of the youths he worked with were gang members who had committed homicide.

One fourteen-year-old boy in his program had shot and killed an innocent teenager to prove himself to his gang. At the trial, the victim's mother sat impassively silent until the end, when the youth was convicted of the killing. After the verdict was announced, she stood up slowly and stared directly at him and stated, "I'm going to kill you." Then the youth was taken away to serve several years in the juvenile facility.

After the first half year the mother of the slain child went to visit his killer. He had been living on the streets before the killing, and she was the only visitor he'd had. For a time they talked, and when she left she gave him some money for cigarettes. Then she started step by step to visit him more regularly, bringing food and small gifts. Near the end of his three-year sentence she asked him what he would be doing when he got out. He was confused and very uncertain, so she offered to set him up with a job at a friend's company. Then she inquired about where he would live, and since he had no family to return to, she offered him temporary use of the spare room in her home.

For eight months he lived there, ate her food, and worked at the job. Then one evening she called him into the living room to talk. She sat down opposite him and waited. Then she started,

"Do you remember in the courtroom when I said I was going to kill you?"

"I sure do," he replied.

"Well, I did," she went on. "I did not want the boy who could kill my son for no reason to remain alive on this earth. I wanted him to die. That's why I started to visit you and bring you things. That's why I got you the job and let you live here in my house. That's how I set about changing you. And that old boy, he's gone. So now I want to ask you, since my son is gone, and that killer is gone, if you'll stay here. I've got room, and I'd like to adopt you if you let me." And she became the mother of her son's killer, the mother he never had.

Our own story may not be so dramatic, yet we have all been betrayed.

We must each start where we are. In large and small ways, in our own family and community, we will be asked to patiently forgive over and over.

~ Do not ignore the effect of each wise action saying, "This will come to nothing." Just as by the gradual fall of raindrops the water jar is filled, so in time the wise become replete with good.

Dhammapada

A Meditation on Forgiveness

There is a formal meditation practice that can help us cultivate the capacity to forgive. In this we ask for and extend forgiveness in three directions. In a Buddhist monastery one might repeat this practice hundreds of times until it becomes natural to the heart.

Let yourself sit comfortably, allowing your eyes to close and your breath to be natural and easy. Let your body and mind relax. Breathing gently into the area of your heart, let yourself feel all the barriers you have erected and the emotions you have carried because you have not forgiven — not forgiven yourself, not forgiven others. Let yourself feel the pain of keeping your heart closed. Breathing softly, begin reciting the following words, letting the images and feelings that come up grow deeper as you repeat them.

Forgiveness from others:

There are many ways that I have hurt and harmed others, have betrayed or abandoned them, caused them suffering, knowingly or unknowingly, out of my pain, fear, anger, and confusion.

Let yourself remember and visualize the ways you have hurt others. See the pain you have caused out of your own fear and confusion. Feel your own sorrow and regret. Sense that finally you can release this burden and ask for forgiveness. Take as much time as you need to picture each memory that still burdens your heart. And then as each person comes to mind, gently say:

I ask for your forgiveness, I ask for your forgiveness.

Just as I have caused suffering to others, there are many ways that I have hurt and harmed myself. I have betrayed or abandoned myself many times in thought, word, or deed, knowingly or unknowingly.

Feel your own precious body and life. Let yourself see the ways you have hurt or harmed yourself. Picture them, remember them. Feel the sorrow you have carried from this and sense that you can release these burdens. Extend forgiveness for each act of harm, one by one. Repeat to yourself:

For the ways I have hurt myself through action or inaction, out of fear, pain, and confusion, I now extend a full and heartfelt forgiveness. I forgive myself, I forgive myself.

FORGIVENESS FOR THOSE WHO HAVE HURT
OR HARMED YOU:

There are many ways I have been harmed by others,
abused or abandoned, knowingly or unknowingly,
in thought, word, or deed.

We each have been betrayed.
Let yourself picture and remember the
many ways this is true. Feel the sorrow
you have carried from this past. Now sense
that you can release this burden of pain by
gradually extending forgiveness as your
heart is ready. Recite to yourself:

I remember the many ways others have hurt,
wounded, or harmed me, out of fear, pain, confusion,
and anger. I have carried this pain in my heart long
enough. To the extent that I am ready, I offer you
forgiveness. To those who have caused me harm,
I offer my forgiveness, I forgive you.

Let yourself gently repeat these three directions for forgiveness until you feel a release in your heart. For some great pains you may not feel a release; instead, you may experience again the burden and the anguish or anger you have held. Touch this softly. Be forgiving of yourself for not being ready to let go and move on. Forgiveness cannot be forced; it cannot be artificial. Simply continue the practice and let the words and images work gradually in their own way. In time you can make the forgiveness meditation a regular part of your life, letting go of the past and opening your heart to each new moment with a wise lovingkindness.

Letting go, grieving, and reconciliation are three additional practices that complement the work of forgiveness. Each offers a wise and simple form, a gracious language to encourage the heart to let go, to heal, and to come to rest.

Let your own intuition guide you as to which of these meditations to practice. Stay with it as long as it serves you, then return when you are ready to the ongoing practice of forgiveness.

A Meditation on Letting Go

~ If you let go a little
you will have a little happiness.
If you let go a lot
you will have a lot of happiness.
If you let go completely
you will be free.

Ajahn Chah

One of the essential tasks for living a wise life is letting go. Letting go is the path to freedom. It is only by letting go of the hopes, the fears, the pain, the past, the stories that have a hold on us that we can quiet our mind and open our heart.

We do not need to fear letting go. We can trust the courage and vulnerability of our heart to meet life as it is; we can rest kindly where we are. As we let go, the tender ground of honesty, healing, and love will carry us through the ever-changing world.

Remember, letting go does not mean losing the knowledge we have gained from the past.

The knowledge of the past stays with us. To let go is to release the images and emotions, the grudges and fears, the clingings and disappointments of the past that bind our spirit. Like emptying a cup, letting go leaves us free to receive, refreshed, sensitive, and awake.

Letting go is not the same as aversion, struggling to get rid of something. We cannot genuinely let go of what we resist. What we resist and fear secretly follows us even as we push it away. To let go of fear or trauma, we need to acknowledge just how it is. We need to feel it fully and accept that it is so. It is as it is. Letting go begins with letting be.

When we learn to let things be, they gradually lose their power; they cease to disturb us.

As we allow what is true, space comes into the body and mind; we breathe and soften and come to rest. In accepting it, we become free. Then we can ask: "Do I have to continue to replay this story? Do I have to hold on to these losses, these feelings? Is it time to let this go?" The heart will know.

There is an organic cycle to letting go. We will feel it as a wisdom that knows it is time to move on, to release the past and tenderly return to the present. When we let go we return to an honest and simple openness.

Let yourself sit comfortably and quietly. Bring a kindly attention to your body and breath. Relax. Let yourself be settled in the ground of the present.

Now bring into awareness the story, the situation, the feelings, the reactions that it is time to let go of. Name them gently (betrayal, sadness, anxiety, etc.) and allow them the space to be, to float without resistance, held in a heart of compassion. Continue to breathe. Ask yourself if it is indeed wise to release this past. Feel the benefit, the ease that will come from this letting go. Say to yourself, *Let go, Let go,* gently over and over.

Soften the body and heart and let any feelings that arise drain out of you into the earth. Sense how the feelings can be released like water draining out of a tub. Feel the space that comes as you let go, how the heart softens and the body opens.

Now direct the mind to envision the future where this situation has been released. Sense the freedom, the innocence, the ease that this letting go can bring. Say to yourself, *Let go,* several more times. Sit quietly and notice if the feelings return. Each time they return, breathe softly as if to bow to them, and say kindly, *I've let you go.*

The images and feelings may come back many times, yet as you continue to practice, they will eventually fade. Gradually the mind will come to trust the space of letting go. Gradually the heart will be easy and you will be free.

A Meditation on Grief

~ When after heavy rain the storm clouds
   disperse, is it not that they've wept
   themselves clear to the end?

Ghalib

Grief is one of the heart's natural responses
to loss. When we grieve we allow ourselves
to feel the truth of our pain, the measure
of betrayal or tragedy in our life. By
our willingness to mourn, we slowly
acknowledge, integrate, and accept the
truth of our losses. Sometimes the best
way to let go is to grieve.

It takes courage to grieve, to honor the
pain we carry. We can grieve in tears or in
meditative silence, in prayer or in song. In
touching the pain of recent and long-held
griefs, we come face to face with our genuine
human vulnerability, with helplessness and
hopelessness. These are the storm clouds of
the heart.

Most traditional societies offer ritual and communal support to help people move through grief and loss. We need to respect our tears. Without a wise way to grieve, we can only soldier on, armored and unfeeling, but our hearts cannot learn and grow from the sorrows of the past.

To meditate on grief, let yourself sit, alone or with a comforting friend. Take the time to create an atmosphere of support. When you are ready, begin by sensing your breath. Feel your breathing in the area of your chest. This can help you become present to what is within you. Take one hand and hold it gently on your heart as if you were holding a vulnerable human being. You are.

As you continue to breathe, bring to mind the loss or pain you are grieving. Let the story, the images, the feelings come naturally. Hold them gently. Take your time. Let the feelings come layer by layer, a little at a time.

Keep breathing softly, compassionately. Let whatever feelings are there, pain and tears, anger and love, fear and sorrow, come as they will. Touch them gently. Let them unravel out of your body and mind. Make space for any images that arise. Allow the whole story. Breathe and hold it all with tenderness and compassion. Kindness for it all, for you and for others.

The grief we carry is part of the grief of the world. Hold it gently. Let it be honored. You do not have to keep it in anymore. You can let go into the heart of compassion; you can weep.

Releasing the grief we carry is a long, tear-filled process. Yet it follows the natural intelligence of the body and heart. Trust it, trust the unfolding. Along with meditation, some of your grief will want to be written, to be cried out, to be sung, to be danced. Let the timeless wisdom within you carry you through grief to an open heart.

A Meditation on Reconciliation

In Buddhist monasteries when conflict arises, the monks and nuns are encouraged to undertake a formal practice of reconciliation. They begin with this simple intention: No matter what the hurt within us, we can seek to be reconciled. Even if we cannot or should not speak to the other, we can find the courage to hold reconciliation and goodwill in our own heart. We can do our part toward the healing of the world.

To recite the intention of reconciliation is to willingly plant a seed of reconnection and love in our heart. As we repeat each phrase, we turn our intention to the possibility of restoring harmony where suffering has set us apart. We begin to build a bridge of tenderness to those who have been separated by pain and fear.

Let yourself sit in a comfortable posture.
Bring your attention gently to your body
and breath. Stay with the breath until you feel
settled and present. Then bring into awareness
the benefits of reconciliation and healing for
all those who have been estranged and set
apart.

We begin within the family because the
family is where we are most vulnerable
and can most easily be hurt. If we cannot
be reconciled here, we will never find
reconciliation with the world.

Picture each person and group named as
you go through this practice. Recite each
simple phrase, one category at a time. Feel
the distance and pain between them. Hold the
tender possibility of restoring love between
them. Know that simply expressing the heart's
willingness to seek reconciliation turns our
life toward peace.

Breathe gently. Slowly recite the following intentions, allowing time to sense the reconnection of each:

May all mothers and sons be reconciled.
May all mothers and daughters be reconciled.
May all fathers and sons be reconciled.
May all fathers and daughters be reconciled.
May all sisters and brothers be reconciled.
May all husbands and wives be reconciled.
May all partners and lovers be reconciled.
May all family members be reconciled.
May all employers and employees be reconciled.
May all community members be reconciled.
May all friends be reconciled.
May all women be reconciled.
May all men be reconciled.
May all men and women be reconciled.
May all religions be reconciled.
May all races be reconciled.
May all nations be reconciled.
May all peoples be reconciled.
May all creatures be reconciled.
May all beings of every form be reconciled.

Lovingkindness

The greatest protection in all the world is lovingkindness.

Buddha

Love is a blessed mystery.

It is like gravity: vast, invisible, the unstoppable force that connects all things.

We long for this love.
We long to love and to be loved.
Wherever we are,
we can awaken to it.

Like a caring mother
   holding and guarding the life
   of her only child,
   so with a boundless heart
   of lovingkindness,
   hold yourself and all beings
   as your beloved children.

Buddha

Lovingkindness offers care and well-wishing
to another without expectation or demand.
There is no distance between their well-being
and our own.

True love is trustworthy. Our love for others
is an expression of our trust in love itself. No
matter what happens, we can still love.

Love creates a communion with life. Love expands us, connects us, sweetens us, ennobles us.

Love springs up in tender concern, it blossoms into caring action. It makes beauty out of all we touch. In any moment we can step beyond our small self and embrace each other as beloved parts of a whole.

In the end, when we look at our life,
the questions will be simple:
Did I live fully?
Did I love well?

If I speak with the tongues of men and of angels, but have not love, I am become as sounding brass or a clanging gong. And if I have the gift of prophecy, and know all knowledge; and if I have all faith, so as to move mountains, but have not love, I am nothing.

1 Corinthians 13:1–2

At times we feel we cannot love.

Because of our confusion and the pain we carry, because of the suffering around us, our love is buried.

In spite of this history, we must learn to find love again, in our body and heart, in our community, in all things.

Without love our creative spirit will dry up.

~ An ulcer is an unkissed imagination taking its revenge for having been jilted. It is an undanced dance, an unpainted watercolor, an unwritten poem.

John Ciardi

Our society has forgotten to teach love.

In the words of John Gatto, New York City Teacher of the Year:

~ Think of the things that are killing us as a nation: drugs, brainless competition, recreational sex, the pornography of violence, gambling, alcohol, and the worst pornography of all — lives devoted to buying things, accumulation as a religion.

Even in terrible times we must learn to love.

~ We all carry within us our places of exile, our crimes, our ravages. Our task is not to unleash them on the world; it is to transform them in ourselves and others.

Albert Camus

Resentment hurts us.

~ Whatever is begun in anger,
ends in shame.

Benjamin Franklin

Our time is too precious
not to love.

~ Knowing life is short,
how can we quarrel?

Buddha

The ground of love is found beyond judgment
and blame.

~   If only it were all so simple! If only there
were evil people somewhere else insidiously
committing evil deeds, and it were simply
necessary to separate them from the rest of
us and destroy them. But the line dividing
good and evil cuts through the heart of
every human being. And who is willing
to destroy a piece of his own heart?

Alexander Solzhenitsyn

THESE UNDERSTANDINGS CAN HELP:

Hate is the first and most obvious enemy of
love. Hate hardens the heart. It holds tight to
our pain and our anger so that the other is cast
as inhuman. Hate disfigures our spirit.

~ Never succumb to the temptation of
becoming bitter. As you press for justice,
be sure to move with dignity and discipline,
using only the instruments of Love.

Martin Luther King Jr.

The other great enemy of love is fear.

Fear contracts the heart. Its worries and anxieties stop the flow of love.

Do we really want to live in fear?

As the Persian poet Hafiz kindly puts it:

~ Fear is the cheapest room in the house. I'd like to see you in better living conditions.

There are also more subtle enemies of love. These imitations of love are attachment and expectation.

When attachment arises in the place of love, it sees the other as separate; it grasps and needs. Attachment is conditional; it seeks control and it fears loss. Ask your heart if attachment has replaced love. If we speak to our heart, it will always tell us the truth.

Expectation is another imitation of love. We care for another, but we really want them to be some other way. Attachment to our hopes and desires, to our subtle expectations destroys the tender space of love. Even the most benevolent expectations can feel like pressure and judgment to another.

Love is generous without need. It is fulfilling in itself. It is courageous. Love offers kindness with no requirement for return.

LOVE IS NOT WEAK.

In this world there are two great sources of strength. One rests with those who are not afraid to kill. The other rests with those who are not afraid to love.

~ If our cause is a mighty one, and surely peace on earth in these days is the great issue, and if we are opposing the powers of destruction, of annihilation, and working on the side of life, then surely we must use our greatest weapon — the forces of love that are in each one of us. To stand on the side of life we must give up our own lives.

Dorothy Day

Love is based on our capacity to trust in a reality beyond fear, to trust a timeless truth bigger than all our difficulties.

Love is without demands.

Sometimes love means standing firm.
Sometimes love means letting go.
Sometimes love means letting be.
Love blossoms whenever we step beyond our fears and rest in the generosity of the heart.

In our closest relationships, where we are most vulnerable, love is not always easy.

Once when Mother Teresa was being interviewed for the British Broadcasting Corporation, the interviewer remarked that in some ways a life of service might be easier for her than for us ordinary householders. After all, he pointed out, she had no possessions, no car, no insurance, and no husband.

"That is not true," she replied. "I am married too." She held up the ring that nuns in her order wear to symbolize their wedding to Christ. Then she added, "And he can be very difficult sometimes!"

If it was difficult for Mother Teresa, it will be difficult for us all at times.

Love is not sentimental.

~ An honorable human relationship, that is, one in which two people have the right to use the word *love,* is a process of deepening the truths they can tell each other. It is important to do this because it breaks down human self-delusion and isolation.

Adrienne Rich

Yet love is very simple.

In understanding lovingkindness, as the Dalai Lama says, "Perhaps it is best to put the emphasis on kindness."

Whether we meet the world with a loving heart or not will determine what we find:

A stranger walked toward the gates of a new city. By the side of the road sat an old wise woman who hailed the traveler: "Welcome."

"What kind of people are they who live here?" the traveler asked.

"How did you find them in the home city you left?" asked the wise woman.

"They were gossips, mean-spirited, and often selfish. Difficult to get along with."

"You'll find the people of this city to be likewise."

Later a second stranger passed by and was welcomed by the old woman.

"What kind of people are they who live here?" the second traveler asked.

"How did you find them in your home city?"

"They were fine people — industrious, open-minded, and easy to get along with."

"You'll find the people of this city to be likewise."

Love begins in the smallest ways.

~ During my second month of nursing school, our professor gave us a pop quiz. I was a conscientious student and had breezed through the questions until I read the last one: "What is the first name of the woman who cleans the school?"

Surely this was some kind of joke. I had seen the cleaning woman several times. She was tall, dark-haired, a woman in her fifties, but how would I know her name? I handed in my paper, leaving the last question blank.

Before class ended, one student asked if the last question would count toward our quiz grade. "Absolutely," said the professor. "In your careers you will meet many people. All are significant. They deserve your attention and care, even if all you do is smile and say hello."

I've never forgotten that lesson. I also learned her name was Dorothy.

Joanne C. Jones

How far you go in life depends on your being tender with the young, compassionate with the aged, sympathetic with the striving, and tolerant of the weak and the strong. Because someday you will have been all of these.

George Washington Carver

With lovingkindness we see with the heart:

~ Saints are what they are not because their sanctity makes them admirable to others, but because the gift of sainthood makes it possible for them to admire everyone else.

Thomas Merton

When love moves through us it inspires all we do.

~ The outer work will never be puny
if the inner work is great.

Meister Eckhart

Since the time of the Buddha, people have
recited the many blessings that come from
cultivating the power of a loving heart.
Here are some of them:

Your dreams become sweet.
You fall asleep easily.
You waken contented.
Your thoughts are pleasant.
Your health improves.
Angels and devas will love and protect you.
Animals will sense your love and not harm you.
People will welcome you everywhere.
Your babies will be happy.
If you lose things, they will be returned.
If you fall off a cliff, a tree will be there to
    catch you.
The world will be more peaceful around you.

True love is unconquerable and irresistible,
and it will go on gathering power and
spreading itself until it transforms everyone
it touches.

Meher Baba

Extend your lovingkindness so that it embraces the whole of humanity, and the whole of the world . . .

~ What is man without the beasts? If all the beasts were gone, men would die from a great loneliness of spirit, for whatever happens to the beasts also happens to man.

Chief Seattle

. . . Even to the smallest creatures.

~ A bug crawls over the paper.
Leave him be.
We need all the readers we can get.

Lloyd Reynolds

MAKE CERTAIN TO INCLUDE YOURSELF.

One of the greatest blocks to lovingkindness is our own sense of unworthiness. If we leave ourselves out of the circle of love and compassion, we have misunderstood.

Love and compassion must begin with kindness
  toward ourselves.

~ You can search the whole universe
    and not find a single being
    more worthy of love than yourself.
    Since each and every person
    is so precious to themselves,
    let the self-respecting
    harm no other being.
                        Buddha

Lovingkindness gives birth to a natural
compassion. The compassionate heart
holds the pain and sorrow of our life and
of all beings with mercy and tenderness.

~ It is this tender heart that has the power
to transform the world.

Chögyam Trungpa

Compassion arises naturally as the quivering of the heart in the face of pain, ours and another's. True compassion is not limited by the separateness of pity, nor by the fear of being overwhelmed. When we come to rest in the great heart of compassion, we discover a capacity to bear witness to, suffer with, and hold dear with our own vulnerable heart the sorrows and beauties of the world.

~ Loving compassion is like sunlight, awakening and bringing joy to beings. Its beauty is like a rainbow, lifting the hearts of all who see it.

Tarthang Tulku

Love and compassion appear as selfless service. Yet in love we do not serve the other, we serve "us."

Love's communion brings us together in a whole. Compassion does not see the world's pain and sorrow as other; it is shared, it is ours.

When we allow our shared vulnerability and humanness, love and compassion are as natural as our breath, and without hesitation we act to help.

~ Compassion is a verb.

Thich Nhat Hanh

COMPASSION IS ALL AROUND US.

As the World Trade Center burned, one man
slowly lowered a colleague in a wheelchair
one step at a time down sixty-eight floors.
They got out in time.

Another offered wet paper towels as smoke
masks to hundreds who descended before
him.

As office workers poured out, teams of
firemen and police rushed in with brave hearts
and great compassion.

In every place of suffering around the globe,
there are those who have discovered the good
heart's capacity to love, and who are willing to
tend to the sorrows of the world as their own.

The loving heart cannot distinguish between large and small matters; all are worthy of love.

~ The scope of selfless service is not limited to great gestures, heroic acts, and huge donations to public institutions. They also serve who express their love in little things. A word that gives courage to a broken heart or a smile that brings hope in the midst of gloom has as much claim to be regarded as service as difficult sacrifices and heroic self-denials. A glance that wipes out bitterness from the heart is also service, although there may be no thought of service in it.

When taken by themselves, all these things seem to be small, but life is made up of such small things. If these small things were ignored, life would be not only unbeautiful but unbearable.

Meher Baba

A gesture of love can transform our day.

The patrons sit at a communal log table and each finds before his plate a modest bottle of wine. Before the meal begins, a man will pour his wine not into his own glass but into his neighbor's. And his neighbor will return the gesture, filling the first man's empty glass. In an economic sense, nothing has happened. No one has any more wine than he did to begin with. But a loving community has appeared where there was none before.

Love and compassion are not the possession of any group or religious system. They are woven into our human spirit and our very cells. The only nourishment they require is our intimate and heartfelt attention.

~ The emergence and blossoming of understanding, love, and intelligence has nothing to do with any tradition — no matter how ancient or impressive — it has nothing to do with time. It happens completely on its own when a human being questions, wonders, listens, and looks without getting stuck in fear. When self-concern is quiet, in abeyance, heaven and earth are open.

Toni Packer

Lovingkindness gives us the capacity to care
for and bless whatever is before us. It is a
freedom and happiness with no cause, fulfilled
and sufficient in itself. From its open heart
love brings a generous spirit to each moment
and each encounter.

There is no hardship and no difficulty that
enough love cannot conquer, no distance
that enough love cannot span, no barrier
that enough love cannot overcome.

I stand by the bed where a young woman lies, her face postoperative, her mouth twisted in palsy, clownish. A tiny twig of the facial nerve, the one to the muscles of her mouth, has been severed. She will be thus from now on. As surgeon, I had followed with religious fervor the curve of her flesh, I promise you that. Nevertheless, to remove the tumor in her cheek, I had to cut the little nerve.

Her young husband is in the room. He stands on the opposite side of the bed, and together they seem to dwell in the evening lamplight, isolated from me, private. "Who are they," I ask myself, "he and this wry mouth who gaze and touch each other so generously?"

The woman speaks:

"Will my mouth always be like this?" she asks.

"Yes," I say. "It is because the nerve was cut."

She nods, is silent. But the young man smiles.

"I like it," he says. "It's kind of cute."

All at once I know who he is. I understand, and I lower my gaze. One is not bold in an encounter with a god. Unmindful of my presence, he bends to kiss her crooked mouth, and I'm so close I can see how he twists his own lips to accommodate hers, to show her that their kiss still works.

I remember that the gods appeared in ancient Greece as mortals, and I hold my breath and let the wonder in.

Dr. Richard Selzer

Love can only be found where we are. Love is
"nearer than near."

~ Are you looking for the Holy One?
I am in the next seat.
My shoulder is against yours.

Kabir

There is an innocence in love, a wholehearted
pleasure and delight.

~ Once a little boy sent me a charming card
with a little drawing. I loved it. I answer
all my children's letters — sometimes very
hastily — but this one I lingered over. I sent
him a card and I drew a picture of a Wild
Thing on it. I wrote, "Dear Jim: I loved your
card."

Then I got a letter back from his mother
and she said, "Jim loved your card so much
he ate it."

That to me was one of the highest
compliments I've ever received. He didn't
care that it was an original Maurice Sendak
drawing or anything. He saw it, he loved it,
he ate it.

Maurice Sendak

Love is more than an ideal. It is warm, generous, direct, and immediate.

~ If one is to do good, it must be done in the minute particulars. General good is the plea of the hypocrite, the flatterer, and the scoundrel.

William Blake

Love does not grandstand. Like water, it is humble and unstoppable.

Love does not try to fix the whole world. It is enough to plant seeds of kindness and justice everywhere we can.

~ I never look at the masses as my responsibility. I look at the individual. I can only love one person at a time. I can only feed one person at a time. Just one, just one . . . So you begin — I begin.

I picked up one person — maybe if I didn't pick up that one person, I wouldn't have picked up forty-two thousand.

The whole work is only a drop in the ocean. But if I didn't put that drop in, the ocean would be one drop less. Same thing for you, same thing in your family, same thing in the community where you live. Just begin . . . one, one, one.

Mother Teresa

O Nobly Born, remember your own loving heart. Trust it, honor it, follow it. It will bring you peace.

~ I am larger and better than I thought.
I did not think I held so much goodness.

Walt Whitman

A Meditation on Lovingkindness

This meditation uses words, images, and feelings to evoke a lovingkindness and friendliness toward oneself and others. With each recitation of the phrases, we are expressing an intention, planting the seeds of loving wishes over and over in our heart.

With a loving heart as the background, all that we attempt, all that we encounter will open and flow more easily.

You can begin the practice of lovingkindness by meditating for fifteen or twenty minutes in a quiet place. Let yourself sit in a comfortable fashion. Let your body rest and be relaxed. Let your heart be soft. Let go of any plans and preoccupations.

Begin with yourself. Breathe gently, and recite inwardly the following traditional phrases directed to your own well-being. You begin with yourself because without loving yourself it is almost impossible to love others.

May I be filled with lovingkindness.
May I be safe from inner and outer dangers.
May I be well in body and mind.
May I be at ease and happy.

As you repeat these phrases, picture yourself as you are now, and hold that image in a heart of lovingkindness. Or perhaps you will find it easier to picture yourself as a young and beloved child. Adjust the words and images in any way you wish. Create the exact phrases that best open your heart of kindness. Repeat these phrases over and over again, letting the feelings permeate your body and mind. Practice this meditation for a number of weeks, until the sense of lovingkindness for yourself grows.

Be aware that this meditation may at times feel mechanical or awkward. It can also bring up feelings contrary to lovingkindness, feelings of irritation and anger. If this happens, it is especially important to be patient and kind toward yourself, allowing whatever arises to be received in a spirit of friendliness and kind affection.

When you feel you have established some stronger sense of lovingkindness for yourself, you can then expand your meditation to include others. After focusing on yourself for five or ten minutes, choose a benefactor, someone in your life who has loved or truly cared for you. Picture this person and carefully recite the same phrases:

May you be filled with lovingkindness.
May you be safe from inner and outer dangers
May you be well in body and mind.
May you be at ease and happy.

Let the image and feelings you have for your benefactor support the meditation. Whether the image or feelings are clear or not does not matter. In meditation they will be subject to change. Simply continue to plant the seeds of loving wishes, repeating the phrases gently no matter what arises.

Expressing gratitude to our benefactors is a natural form of love. In fact, some people find lovingkindness for themselves so hard, they begin their practice with a benefactor. This too is fine. The rule in lovingkindness practice is to follow the way that most easily opens your heart.

When lovingkindness for your benefactor has developed, you can gradually begin to include other people you love in your meditation. Picturing each beloved person, recite inwardly the same phrases, evoking a sense of lovingkindness for each person in turn.

After this you can include others: Spend some time wishing well to a wider circle of friends. Then gradually extend your meditation to picture and include community members, neighbors, people everywhere, animals, all beings, the whole earth.

Finally, include the difficult people in your life, even your enemies, wishing that they too may be filled with lovingkindness and peace. This will take practice. But as your heart opens, first to loved ones and friends, you will find that in the end you won't want to close it to anyone.

Lovingkindness can be practiced anywhere. You can use this meditation in traffic jams, in buses, and on airplanes. As you silently practice this meditation among people, you will immediately feel a wonderful connection with them — the power of lovingkindness. It will calm your mind and keep you connected to your heart.

OTHER PRACTICES THAT SUPPORT LOVINGKINDNESS:

Compassion, gratitude, and joy are companions to the work of lovingkindness. Compassion practice offers a conscious vehicle for our natural concern for the sorrows of the world. Gratitude and joy balance the sorrows of compassion and awaken in us a generous and gracious spirit.

Use these meditations intuitively, drawing upon each as your heart tells you.

A Meditation on Compassion

The human heart has the extraordinary capacity to transform the sorrows of life into a great stream of compassion. Compassion proclaims the power of the tender and merciful heart in the face of the sufferings of the world. It arises whenever we allow our heart to be touched by the pain and need of another.

To cultivate compassion, let yourself sit in a centered and quiet way. Breathe softly and feel your body, your heartbeat, the life within you. Feel how you treasure your own life, how you guard yourself in the face of your sorrows. After some time, bring to mind someone close to you whom you dearly love. Picture them and feel your natural caring for them. Notice how you hold them in your heart. Then let yourself be aware of their sorrows, their measure of suffering in life. Feel how your heart opens to wish them well, to extend comfort, to share in their pain and meet it with compassion.

This is the natural response of the heart. To open still further, begin reciting the phrases:

May you be held in compassion.
May you be free from pain and sorrow.
May you be at peace.

Continue reciting all the while you are holding them in your heart.

After you learn to feel your deep caring for this person close to you, turn your compassionate heart toward yourself and the measure of sorrows you carry. For a time recite the phrases:

May I be held in compassion.
May I be free from pain and sorrow.
May I be at peace.

Now, one person at a time, extend your compassion to others you know. Picture loved ones, one after another. Hold the image of each in your heart, be aware of their difficulties, and wish them well.

May you be held in compassion.
May you be free from pain and sorrow.
May you be at peace.

Now you can open your compassion further: to the suffering of your friends, to your neighbors, to your community, to all who suffer, to difficult people, to your enemies, and finally to the brotherhood and sisterhood of all beings.

Let yourself feel how the beauty of every being brings you joy and how the suffering of any being makes you weep. Feel your tenderhearted connection with all life and its creatures.

Now let your heart become a transformer for the sorrows of the world. Feel the breath in the area of your heart, as if you could breathe gently in and out of your heart. Feel the kindness of your heart and envision that with each breath you can breathe in pain and breathe out compassion.

Start to breathe in the sorrows of living beings. With each in-breath, let their sorrows touch your heart and turn into compassion. With each out-breath, wish all living beings well, and extend your caring and merciful heart to them.

May you be held in compassion.
May you be free of pain and sorrow.
May you be at peace.

As you breathe, begin to envision your heart as a purifying fire that can receive the pains of the world and transform them into the light and warmth of compassion. Be gentle with yourself. Let the fire of your heart burn gently in your chest. If you struggle in any way, let the fire burn away all the obstacles to compassion so your heart returns to its naturally generous, open, fearless state.

When you feel your practice is ready, breathe in the sorrows of those who are hungry. Breathe in the sorrows of those who are caught in war. Breathe in the sorrows of ignorance. With each out-breath, picture living beings everywhere and breathe out the healing balm of compassion. With every gentle in-breath, over and over, let the sorrows of every form of life touch your heart. With every out-breath, over and over, extend the mercy and healing of compassion. Like the mother of the world, bring the world into your heart. Invite all beings to touch you with each breath in. Embrace all beings in compassion with each breath out.

After some time, sit quietly and let your breath and heart rest naturally, as a center of compassion in the midst of the world.

Work with compassion practice intuitively. At times it may feel difficult, as though we might be overwhelmed by the pain. Remember, we are not trying to "fix" the pain of the world, only to meet it with a compassionate heart. Relax and be gentle. Breathe. It is not necessary to armor and shut down.

If you find difficulties, shift your attention to your own well-being. Hold yourself in compassion, be patient. Then choose a person who evokes this same tender compassion in an easy and natural way. Gradually learn to trust the opening of the heart. Over time you will find a deepening capacity to open to all that life brings. Whenever you encounter the sorrows of the world and find them calling to your heart, take the time to return to compassion.

A Meditation on Gratitude and Joy

~ If we cannot be happy in spite of our difficulties, what good is our spiritual practice?

Maha Ghosananda

Buddhist monks begin each day with a chant of gratitude for the blessings of their life. Native American elders begin each ceremony with grateful prayers to mother earth and father sky, to the four directions, to the animal, plant, and mineral brothers and sisters who share our earth and support our life. In Tibet, the monks and nuns even offer prayers of gratitude for the suffering they have been given: "Grant that I might have enough suffering to awaken in me the deepest possible compassion and wisdom."

The aim of spiritual life is to awaken a joyful freedom, a benevolent and compassionate heart in spite of everything.

Gratitude is a gracious acknowledgment of all that sustains us, a bow to our blessings, great and small, an appreciation of the moments of good fortune that sustain our life every day. We have so much to be grateful for.

Gratitude is confidence in life itself. In it, we feel how the same force that pushes grass through cracks in the sidewalk invigorates our own life.

Gratitude gladdens the heart. It is not sentimental, not jealous, nor judgmental. Gratitude does not envy or compare. Gratitude receives in wonder the myriad offerings of the rain and the earth, the care that supports every single life.

As gratitude grows it gives rise to joy. We experience the courage to rejoice in our own good fortune and in the good fortune of others.

Joy is natural to an open heart. In it, we are not afraid of pleasure. We do not mistakenly believe it is disloyal to the suffering of the world to honor the happiness we have been given.

Like gratitude, joy gladdens the heart. We can be joyful for people we love, for moments of goodness, for sunlight and trees, and for the breath within our breast. And as our joy grows we finally discover a happiness without cause. Like an innocent child who does not have to do anything to be happy, we can rejoice in life itself, in being alive.

Let yourself sit quietly and at ease. Allow your body to be relaxed and open, your breath natural, your heart easy. Begin the practice of gratitude by feeling how year after year you have cared for your own life. Now let yourself begin to acknowledge all that has supported you in this care:

With gratitude I remember the people, animals, plants, insects, creatures of the sky and sea, air and water, fire and earth, all whose joyful exertion blesses my life every day.

With gratitude I remember the care and labor of a thousand generations of elders and ancestors who came before me.

I offer my gratitude for the safety and well-being I have been given.

I offer my gratitude for the blessings of this earth I have been given.

I offer my gratitude for the measure of health I have been given.

I offer my gratitude for the family and friends I have been given.

I offer my gratitude for the community I have been given.

I offer my gratitude for the teachings and lessons I have been given.

I offer my gratitude for the life I have been given.

Just as we are grateful for our blessings, so we can be grateful for the blessings of others.

Continue to breathe gently. Bring to mind someone you care about, someone it is easy to rejoice for. Picture them and feel the natural joy you have for their well-being, for their happiness and success. With each breath, offer them your grateful, heartfelt wishes:

May you be joyful.
   May your happiness increase.
   May you not be separated from great happiness.
   May your good fortune and the causes for your joy and happiness increase.

Sense the sympathetic joy and caring in each phrase. When you feel some degree of natural gratitude for the happiness of this loved one, extend this practice to another person you care about. Recite the same simple phrases that express your heart's intention.

Then gradually open the meditation to include neutral people, difficult people, and even enemies — until you extend sympathetic joy to all beings everywhere, young and old, near and far.

Peace

The human mind can create conflict.
It can also create peace.
To find peace in the world
we must find peace in ourselves.

~ There is no higher happiness
than peace.

Buddha

Within each of us there is
a silence as vast as the universe.
We long for it.
We can return to it.

To make peace
we cannot ignore
war, racism, violence, greed,
the injustice and sufferings
of the world.

They must be confronted
with courage and compassion.
Unless we seek justice
peace will fail.

Yet in whatever we do
we must not let
war, violence, and fear
take over our own heart.

Whatever the situation,
we cannot make peace
unless we ourselves are peaceful.

~ When the crowded refugee boats met with
storms or pirates, if everyone panicked, all
would be lost. But if even one person on the
boat remained calm and centered, it was
enough. They showed the way for everyone
to survive.

Thich Nhat Hanh

There are those who discover they can leave
   behind destructive reactions
   and become patient as the earth,
   unmoved by fires of anger or fear,
   unshaken as a pillar,
   unperturbed as a clear and quiet pool.

Dhammapada

Peace is born out of
equanimity and balance.
Balance is flexibility,
an ability to adjust graciously to change.
Equanimity arises when we
accept the way things are.

~ If you expect your life to be up and down,
your mind will be much more peaceful.

Lama Yeshe

The first step to the knowledge of the wonder and mystery of life is the recognition of the monstrous nature of the earthly human realm as well as its glory, the realization that this is just how it is and that it cannot and will not be changed. Those who think they know — and their name is legion — how the universe could have been had they created it, without pain, without sorrow, without time, without death, are unfit for illumination.

So if you really want to help this world, what you will have to teach is how to live in it. And that no one can do who has not themself learned how to live in the joyful sorrow and sorrowful joy of the knowledge of life as it is.

Joseph Campbell

Praise and blame,
gain and loss,
pleasure and pain,
fame and disrepute
are the eight worldly winds.
They ceaselessly change.

As a mountain is
unshaken by the wind,
so the heart of a wise person
is unmoved
by all the changes on this earth.

Buddha

Embracing both joy and sorrow,
   our heart can remain
   tender and wise.

~ We can walk through
   the darkest night
   with the radiant conviction
   that all things work together
   for the good.

Martin Luther King Jr.

Peace is not an absence
of change or difficulty.
It should not be confused with
withdrawal or indifference to life.
These are imitations of peace,
ways of closing down based on fear.
We must see them for what they are.

Withdrawal removes us from
connectedness,
from openness, from love.
When we withdraw out of fear, we run away.
We believe that by disconnecting from others
we will be safe.
Withdrawal is not true inner peace.

Indifference pretends to create peace, but it is based on not caring, a silent resignation. It is a movement away, a separation fed by a subtle fear of the heart. We pull back, believing that what happens to others is not our concern. Our courage leaves us. Indifference is a misguided way of defending ourselves.

The peace of the heart
  is not emotional resignation,
  but an openness
  that meets the ever-changing world
  with compassion.

  With equanimity
  we can care for all things
  without trying to
  control them.

We can cultivate compassion for others and strive to alleviate suffering in the world, yet still there are many situations we are unable to affect. As the serenity prayer says, "May I have the serenity to accept the things I cannot change, the courage to change the things I can, and the wisdom to know the difference."

Acceptance does not mean inaction.
We may need to respond,
strongly at times.

From a peaceful center
we can respond instead of react.
Unconscious reactions create problems.
Considered responses bring peace.
With a peaceful heart
whatever happens can be met
with wisdom.

Peace is not weak;
it is unshakable.

Grasping too tightly
the things of this world,
attachments arise.

Holding only to how we want it to be,
anger is born.

Not understanding the inevitability of change,
confusion clouds the mind.

~ Meet this transient world
with neither grasping nor fear,
trust the unfolding of life,
and you will attain true serenity.

Bhagavad Gita

True peace comes with the discovery that we can respect the seasons of life with a spacious and undefended heart. In it we learn to trust, to rest in the truth of the way things are, to willingly accept the measure of joy and sorrow we are given.

If you put a spoonful of salt
in a cup of water
it tastes very salty.
If you put a spoonful of salt
in a lake of fresh water
the taste is still pure and clear.

Peace comes when our hearts are
open like the sky,
vast as the ocean.

Do not think that
peace is not possible for you.

I claim to be no more than an average person with less than average ability. I have not the shadow of a doubt that any man or woman can achieve what I have, if he or she would make the same effort and cultivate the same hope and faith.

Gandhi

Yet to find peace
  we have to let go of our struggles,
  to stop making war with life.

~ We human beings are constantly in combat,
    at war to escape the fact of being so limited
    by so many circumstances we cannot
    control. But instead of escaping, we
    continue to create suffering, waging war
    with evil, waging war with good, waging
    war with what is too small, waging war
    with what is too big, waging war with what
    is too short or too long, or right or wrong,
    courageously carrying on the battle.

Ajahn Chah

Let yourself breathe and trust.
It is only by a courageous letting go
that the heart becomes free.
This is called the wisdom of insecurity.

~ Security is mostly a superstition.
It does not exist in nature,
nor do children as a whole experience it.
Avoiding danger is no safer in the long run
than outright exposure.
Life is either a daring adventure
or nothing.

Helen Keller

In the last century, a tourist from America paid a visit to a renowned Polish rabbi, Hofetz Chaim.

He was astonished to see that the rabbi's home was only a simple room filled with books, plus a table and a bench.

"Rabbi," asked the tourist, "where is your furniture?"

"Where is yours?" replied Hofetz Chaim.

"Mine?" asked the puzzled American. "But I'm only passing through."

"So am I," said the rabbi, "so am I."

Tales of the Hasidim

Peace requires us to surrender
our illusions of control.
We can love and care for others
but we cannot possess
our children, lovers, family, or friends.
We can assist them, pray for them, and wish
them well,
yet in the end
their happiness and suffering
depend on their thoughts and actions,
not on our wishes.

Even trying too hard to be good,
we can lose our center.

~ To allow oneself to be carried away by
a multitude of conflicting concerns, to
surrender to too many demands, to commit
oneself to too many projects, to want to
help everyone in everything, is to succumb
to the violence of our times.

Thomas Merton

The truth is,
no matter what course we follow,
difficulties will arise.

In the words of Toni Murden, the first woman
to row solo across the Atlantic Ocean:

~ If you know what it means to be out in the
middle of an ocean by yourself, in the dark,
scared, then it gives you a feel for what
every other human being is going through.
I row an actual ocean. Other people have
just as many obstacles to go through.

Can we accept this truth?

The Lord giveth and
the Lord taketh away.

The ancient words of Ecclesiastes remind us:

~ To everything there is a season
and a time to every purpose under heaven —
a time to be born and a time to die,
a time to plant and a time to reap that
which is planted,
a time to kill and a time to heal,
a time to break down and a time to build up,
a time to weep and a time to laugh,
a time to mourn and a time to dance.

So, too, we are taught by the Tao:

~   There is a time for being ahead,
    a time for being behind;
    a time for being in motion,
    a time for being at rest;
    a time for being vigorous,
    a time for being exhausted;
    a time for being safe,
    a time for being in danger.

    The Master sees things as they are,
    without trying to control them.
    She lets them go their own way,
    and resides at the center of the circle.

To let go does not mean
to get rid of.

To let go means
to let be.

When we let be with compassion,
things come and go
on their own.

We can direct our actions
but not their fruits.

~ The secret of human freedom is to act well,
without attachment to the results.

Bhagavad Gita

As we step out of the way
new things are born.

$\sim$ No seed ever sees the flower.

Zen teaching

Without understanding,
   our worries and thoughts
   create huge, unnecessary problems.

~ My life has been filled with terrible
   misfortunes — most of which never
   happened.

Mark Twain

We know that life changes unexpectedly.
   Though outer events may be difficult,
   the key to our happiness
   is how our mind responds to them.

~ Most people believe the mind to be a
   mirror, more or less accurately reflecting
   the world outside of them, not realizing
   on the contrary that the mind is itself the
   principal element of creation.

Rabindranath Tagore

Mind creates both
the entanglements of the world
and freedom from them.

Yet there is nothing much to it —
it is just thoughts.

Once we recognize that thoughts are empty,
the mind will no longer have the power
to deceive us.

Khyentse Rinpoche

We can be lost in our thoughts and fears.
Or we can remember to breathe,
to soften the heart, to trust.

~ Sometimes I go about
pitying myself
and all the while
I am being carried by great winds
across the sky.

Ojibway Indian

We can struggle with what is.
We can judge and blame
others or ourselves.
Or we can accept what cannot be changed.
Peace comes from
an honorable and open heart
accepting what is true.

Do we want to remain stuck?
Or to release the fearful sense of self
and rest kindly where we are?

The art of living . . . is neither careless drifting on the one hand nor fearful clinging to the past on the other. It consists in being sensitive to each moment, in regarding it as utterly new and unique, in having the mind open and wholly receptive.

Alan Watts

To live here and now you must train yourself:
In the seen there will be just the seen, in the
heard just the heard, in the sensed just the
sensed, in the thought just the thought. That
is the end of sorrow.

Buddha

What would we have to
hold in compassion
to be at peace right now?

What would we have to
let go of
to be at peace right now?

Like a traveler on a train
we can put down our bags.
We can relax our grip
and trust in the unfolding of life.

Do not worry.
There is a web of life
into which we are born,
from which we can never fall.

~ We are caught in an inescapable network
of mutuality, tied in a single garment of
destiny.

Martin Luther King Jr.

We can understand that each of us plays only
a small part, and yet each contributes to
the whole.

~ "Tell me the weight of a snowflake," a
coal-mouse asked a wild dove.

"Nothing more than nothing," was the
answer.

"In that case I must tell you a marvelous
story," the coal-mouse said. "I sat on a
branch of a fir, close to its trunk, when it
began to snow, not heavily, not in a giant
blizzard, no, just like in a dream, without
any violence. Since I didn't have anything
better to do, I counted the snowflakes
settling on the twigs and needles of my
branch. Their number was exactly
3,741,952. When the next snowflake
dropped onto the branch — nothing more
than nothing, as you say — the branch
broke off."

Having said that, the coal-mouse flew
away. The dove, since Noah's time an

authority on change, thought about the story for a while and finally said to herself: "Perhaps there is only one person's voice lacking for peace to come about in the world."

Kurt Kauter

Though I do not believe that a plant will spring up where no seed has been, I have great faith in a seed. Convince me that you have a seed there, and I am prepared to expect wonders.

Henry David Thoreau

We can plant our seeds
and trust.
In this we find our center.

O Nobly Born . . .
plant seeds of compassion
and let go into the spacious awareness
that contains all things.
Be here in the eternal present.
Let this be your resting place,
your safety, your home.

In bullfighting there is a place in the ring where the bull feels safe. If he can reach this place, he stops running and can gather his full strength. He is no longer afraid . . . It is the job of the matador to know where this sanctuary lies, to be sure the bull does not have time to occupy his place of wholeness.

This safe place for a bull is called the *querencia*. For humans the querencia is the safe place in our inner world . . . When a person finds their querencia, in full view of the matador, they are calm and peaceful. Wise. They have gathered their strength around them.

Rachel Naomi Remen

With equanimity we can see clearly.

~ We can make our minds so like still water
that beings gather around us, that they
may see their own images, and so live for
a moment with a clearer perhaps even a
fiercer life because of our quiet.

William Butler Yeats

From this center of stillness
  we can enter life fully,
  yet our heart remains free.

~ A man or woman of knowledge
     sweats and puffs like any ordinary person.
     Yet the folly of their life
     is under control.

Don Juan

A Zen story tells that during a time of civil war in Korea, a certain general led his troops through province after province, overrunning whatever stood in his path. The people of one town, knowing that he was coming and having heard tales of his cruelty, all fled into the mountains. The general arrived in the empty town with his troops and sent them out to search the town. Some of the soldiers came back and reported that only one person remained, a Zen priest. The general strode over to the temple, walked in, pulled out his sword, and said, "Don't you know who I am? I am the one who can run you through without batting an eye."

The Zen master looked back and calmly responded, "And I, sir, am one who can be run through without batting an eye." The general, hearing this, bowed and left.

Wisdom comes when we see
with a vast perspective.
Our life is unfolding
in the timeless galaxies.
We turn with the stars
in cycles of light and dark,
birth and death,
joy and sorrow.

~ Perceive that you are not yet begotten, that
you are in the womb, that you are young,
that you are old, that you have died, that
you are in the world beyond the grave.
Grasp in your mind all this at once, all times
and places, all substances and qualities and
magnitudes together. Then you can begin
to see with the eye of the divine.

Hermes Trismegistus

With a big picture, life becomes play.

~ You are eight years old. It is Sunday evening. You have been granted an extra hour before bed.

The family is playing Monopoly. You have been told you are big enough to join them.

You lose. You are losing continuously. Your stomach cramps with fear. . . . The money pile in front of you is almost gone. Your brothers are snatching all the houses from your streets. The last street is being sold. You have to give in. You have lost.

And suddenly you know that it is only a game. You jump up with joy and you accidentally knock the lamp over. It falls on the floor and drags the teapot with it. The others are angry but you laugh when you go upstairs.

You know, for you have seen the joy of being nothing and having nothing. And knowing that gives an immeasurable freedom.

Janwillem van de Wetering

W e can sense the ever-changing waves around us,
and breathe and relax.
We can rest in the eternal present,
the still point.
We can learn that no matter what happens,
we are home.

~ Now we are ready to look
at something pretty special.
It is a duck riding the ocean
a hundred feet beyond the surf,
as he cuddles in the swells.
There is a big heaving in the Atlantic,
and he is part of it.
He can rest while the Atlantic heaves,
because he rests in the Atlantic.
Probably he doesn't *know*
how large the ocean is.
And neither do you.
But he *realizes* it.
And what does he do, I ask you?

He sits down in it.
He reposes in the immediate
as if it were infinity — which it is.
That is religion, and the duck has it.
How about you?

Donald C. Babcock

The Buddhist teachings remind us
to look upon this fleeting world as:

~ A star at dawn
A flash of lightning in a summer cloud
An echo
A rainbow
A phantom and
A dream.

Diamond Sutra

When we feel
the tentative passing of our days,
life becomes all the more precious:
the luminous gold of a sunset,
the maple tree in autumn,
the gaze of our beloved.

~ There is only one world, the world pressing
against you at this minute. There is only one
minute in which you are alive, this minute
here and now. The only way to live is by
accepting each minute as an unrepeatable
miracle.

Storm Jameson

When we are truly present
  wherever we are,
  we bring peace.

~ She who is centered in the Tao
  can go where she wishes, without danger.
  She perceives the universal harmony,
  even amid great pain,
  because she has found peace in her heart.

Tao Te Ching

Do not be afraid to take a chance
on peace, to teach peace,
to live peace . . .
Peace will be the last word of history.

John Paul II

And all shall be well,
and all manner of thing
shall be well.

Julian of Norwich

A Meditation on Equanimity and Peace

To cultivate the qualities of peace and equanimity, sit in a comfortable posture with your eyes closed. Bring a soft attention to your breath until your body and mind are calm. Reflect for a moment on the benefit of a mind that has balance and equanimity. Sense what a gift it can be to bring a peaceful heart to the world around you. Let yourself feel an inner sense of balance and ease. Then with each breath begin gently repeating such phrases as:

Breathing in, I calm my body.
Breathing out, I calm my mind.
May I be balanced.
May I be at peace.

Stay with these phrases until you feel quiet in your body and mind.

Then broaden the sense of calm into a spacious equanimity. Acknowledge that all created things arise and pass away: joys, sorrows, pleasant and painful events, people, buildings, animals, nations, even whole civilizations. Let yourself rest in the midst of them.

May I learn to see the arising and passing of all things with equanimity and balance.
May I be open and balanced and peaceful.

When you have established a sense of equanimity and peace, begin to picture, one at a time, your loved ones. Carefully recite the same simple phrases:

May you learn to see the arising and passing of all things with equanimity and balance.
May you be open, balanced, and at peace.

Let the image of each loved one be surrounded with peace. Continue as best you can, breathing gently, patiently wishing peace, repeating the phrases no matter what arises.

As the quality of equanimity and peace grows you can gradually expand the meditation to include others. Start with your benefactors, those who have cared for you. Picture each person in turn, reciting inwardly the same phrases, offering a blessing of peace as you continue. Then gradually expand the circle of the meditation to systematically include friends, neighbors, neutral people, animals, all beings, the earth.

May you learn to see the arising and passing of all things with equanimity and balance.
May you be open, balanced, and at peace.

Finally, you can include the difficult people in your life, even your enemies, wishing that they too find equanimity and peace.

As you reflect on each person, it is traditional to acknowledge that all beings are heirs to their own karma. All beings receive the fruits of their actions. Their lives arise and pass away according to the deeds created by them. We can deeply care for them, but in the end we cannot act for them nor let go for them nor love for them. If it is helpful in freeing the heart, you can recite:

Your happiness and suffering depend on your actions and not on my wishes for you.

Reflecting with wisdom on beings and their deeds, you can now picture each one and return to these simple phrases:

May you rest with a peaceful heart.
May you find balance and peace.
May you have compassion and equanimity with all the events of the world.

Continue this practice as long and as often as you wish, breathing and resting the heart in natural great peace.

OTHER PRACTICES THAT SUPPORT EQUANIMITY AND PEACE:

The following meditations support a clear mind and openhearted ease. They invite wisdom, spaciousness, and peace. Let yourself explore each of them. Sense how each image and practice can be a gateway to freedom, a gateway to peace.

Mind like the Ocean

~ Develop a mind that is vast like the water,
where experiences both pleasant and
unpleasant can appear and disappear
without conflict, struggle, or harm.
Rest in a mind like vast water.

Buddha

Sit comfortably and at ease. Let your body
be at rest and your breath natural. Close your
eyes. Take several full breaths and let each one
release. Allow yourself to be still.

Now sense, feel, or imagine that your
mind is like a great ocean. Sense yourself deep
underwater, silent and at ease. Float as if in the
depths of the ocean; relax and rest in the vast
calming water. Notice how waves of sound,
feelings, and thought arise in this ocean, yet
the ocean is untroubled. Let thoughts and
images come and go like waves on the surface.
Let the sounds and sensations float and change
as they will. Let all the experiences in the
meditation arise and pass, moving without
resistance, disappearing without struggle.

Rest in this deep silent peace. Let your mind become like the water, accepting all things, untroubled, still.

Stay this way until you feel genuinely refreshed and peaceful. Then return, gently carrying your stillness back to the world.

Mind like a Mirror

~ Clean the mirror of your mind.
No mind and no mirror to wipe clean.

Zen sayings

Sit comfortably and allow yourself to become
settled, at ease and present on the earth. Take
several full breaths and let each one release
gently. Allow yourself to be at rest.

Now let yourself become quite present,
alert. Imagine your own mind as a vast mirror
just behind you. It is clear, shining, smooth as
glass, perfectly reflective, untarnished by all
that is reflected in it.

See how all the images and thoughts, joys
and sorrows, plans and memories that arise
are simply reflected as they are. No need for
judgment, for grasping or aversion. Thoughts
and feelings, sounds and sensations arise and
are seen in the mirror as images with no
power to harm or disturb.

Rest with a mind like a mirror for some
time, then let yourself return to the world
clear, unreactive, inwardly at peace.

Mind like the Sky

~ Develop a mind that is vast like space,
where experiences both pleasant and
unpleasant can appear and disappear
without conflict, struggle, or harm.
Rest in a mind like vast sky.

Buddha

Sit comfortably and at ease. Let your body
be at rest and your breath natural. Close
your eyes or sit where you can gaze softly
into the distance. Take several full breaths
and let each release gently. Allow yourself
to be still.

Now shift awareness away from the breath.
Begin to listen to the play of sounds around
you. Notice those that are loud and soft, far
and near. Just listen. Notice how all sounds
arise and vanish leaving no trace. Listen for
a time in a relaxed, open way.

As you listen, let yourself sense or imagine that your mind is not limited to your head. Sense that your mind is expanding to be like the sky, open, clear, vast like space. There is no inside or outside. Let the awareness of your mind extend in every direction like the sky.

Now the sounds you hear will arise and pass away in the open space of your own mind. Relax in this openness and just listen. Let the sounds that come and go, far and near, be like clouds in the vast sky of your own awareness. The play of sounds moves through the sky, appearing and disappearing without resistance.

As you rest in this open awareness, notice how thoughts and images also arise and vanish like sounds. Let the thoughts and images come and go without struggle or resistance. Pleasant and unpleasant thoughts, pictures, words, and feelings move unrestricted in the space of mind. Problems, possibilities, joys, and sorrows come and go like clouds in the clear sky of mind.

After a time, let this spacious awareness notice the body. Become aware of how the sensations of breath and body float and change in the same open sky of awareness. The breath breathes itself, it moves like a breeze. The body is not solid. It is felt as areas of hardness and softness, pressure and tingling, warm and cool sensation, all floating in the space of the mind's awareness.

Let the breath move like a breeze. Rest in this openness. Let sensations float and change. Allow all thoughts and images, feelings and sounds to come and go like clouds in the clear open space of awareness.

Finally, pay attention to the awareness itself. Notice how the open space of awareness is naturally clear, transparent, timeless, without conflict, allowing all things, but not limited by them.

"O Nobly Born, remember the pure open sky of your own true nature. Return to it. Trust it. It is home."

May the blessings of these words and practices of forgiveness, lovingkindness, and peace awaken your own inner wisdom and inspire your compassion.

May you be well.
May you be happy.
May you be at peace.
And through the blessing
of your heart
may the world find peace.

Shanti, shanti, shanti.
Peace.

Acknowledgments

I offer gratitude to my teachers and the lineage of the Elders who have offered these teachings so freely. In particular I bow to Maha Ghosananda, the beloved "Gandhi" of Cambodia, because of how faithfully he embodies lovingkindness for so many of us.

The meditations here are representative of traditional Buddhist practices. For their practices of "Mind like Sky" and "The Practice of Reconciliation" I wish to thank and acknowledge Joseph Goldstein and Philip Moffitt respectively. I thank Norman Fischer for his words on gratitude. In the same spirit I thank all my other teaching colleagues for what they have given me.

Toni Burbank, executive editor at Bantam Books, has refined these pages with her usual wise heart and exquisite eye. I could not wish for a better or more supportive editor. I also thank Julie Donovan for her patient transcribing of these words.

As always I learn the most about lovingkindness from my family, my brothers Laurence, Irv, and Kenneth, and my amazing wife Liana and beloved daughter Caroline.

The permissions that follow this acknowledgment are for stories that have been told in many forms. They are part of our universal heritage, for such stories have carried the living wisdom of past generations, retold in childhood, by the side of a fire, in sacred texts, or by a respected teacher. They are almost never "new." They are the stories of our human heart. As best as possible, the permissions below reflect what I could find as current sources, but in the end such stories are gateways we share in common.

For these and the other fine materials herein acknowledged, I gratefully thank the authors and translators.

Sources and Permissions

Grateful acknowledgment is made to the following publishers and authors for the fine material from their books:

Quotation from *Man's Search for Meaning* by Viktor E. Frankl. Revised edition published by Washington Square Press, 1988.

Quotation from *Owning Your Own Shadow* by Robert A. Johnson. Copyright © 1991 by Robert A. Johnson. Published by HarperCollins Publishers, Inc.

From *The Dhammapada: Sayings of the Buddha* translated by Thomas Byron. Reprinted by arrangement with Shambhala Publications, Inc., Boston.

Quotation from *The Drama of the Gifted Child* by Alice Miller. Revised edition published by Basic Books, 1996.

From *The Places that Scare You* by Pema Chödrön. Reprinted by arrangement with Shambhala Publications, Inc., Boston.

From the collection *The Best of Bits and Pieces,* author unknown. Reprinted by arrangement with the Economics Press.

Quotation from *Women and Honor: Some Notes on Lying* by Adrienne Rich. Published by Cleis Press, 1977.

Quotation from *The Gift: Imagination and the Erotic Life of Property* by Lewis Hyde. Published by Vintage Books, 1983.

From *The Gift: Poems by Hafiz, The Great Sufi Master,* by Daniel Ladinsky. Copyright © 1999 by Daniel Ladinsky. Reprinted by permission of the author.

From *Mortal Lessons: Notes on the Art of Surgery* by Richard Selzer. Copyright © 1996 by Richard Selzer. Reprinted by permission of Houghton Mifflin Co.

From *The Kabir Book: 44 of the Ecstatic Poems of Kabir* by Robert Bly. Copyright © 1971, 1977 by Robert Bly. Reprinted by permission of Beacon Press.

Excerpts from *Tao Te Ching,* translated by Stephen Mitchell. Copyright © 1988 by Stephen Mitchell. Reprinted by permission of HarperCollins Publishers, Inc.

From *A Glimpse of Nothingness: Experiences in an American Zen Community* by Janwillem Van De Wetering. Reprinted by arrangement with St. Martin's Press.

About the Author

JACK KORNFIELD was trained as a Buddhist monk in Thailand, Burma, and India and has taught meditation worldwide since 1974. He also holds a Ph.D. in clinical psychology. He is a founder of the Insight Meditation Society and of Spirit Rock Center in northern California. His books include *The Wise Heart, After the Ecstasy, the Laundry, A Path with Heart, Seeking the Heart of Wisdom* (with Joseph Goldstein), *Teachings of the Buddha, Living Dharma, A Still Forest Pool* (with Paul Breiter), and *Soul Food* (with Christina Feldman).

Meditation Classes and Retreats

For information about meditation training and retreats throughout North America, contact:

SPIRIT ROCK MEDITATION CENTER
P.O. Box 169F
Woodacre, CA 94973
(415) 488-0164
www.spiritrock.org